Thank you for reading our book!

We hope you enjoy it and that you will consider sharing it with your friends and family. Whether you are completely new to Bitcoin or you have been around since the early days, we hope this book will inspire you to keep learning, building, and sharing Bitcoin with those you love.

Flo, Brekkie & Simon

In two thousand and eight, when the world was aflame,
A cypherpunk surfaced and refused us his name,
Decentralized money, Satoshi proposed,
And with a paper so white, Bitcoin arose...

Hal Finney believed, and others did too,
In a future with Bitcoin, for me and for you,
A world in which people, no matter how small,
Can interact as sovereigns, once and for all.

Such a world hadn't been, nor would it be,
Until Bitcoin arrived, for you and for me,
But Satoshi's great work, was only the beginning,
There was much left to do, and the dollar was winning...

But what, you may ask, did the dollar do wrong?
It's been working just fine; we've had it so long!
Perhaps it is time, to go for a stroll,
Yes now is the time, to speak of control...

The government tells us our markets are free,
But money's restricted, so how can that be?
If money can't flow, to where it needs go,
Then all of this freedom, is simply a show.

Money is a good, just like clothes or food,
But the State sets the price, how controlling, how rude!
And the day is soon approaching, when cash will be banned,
Freedom will slip away, like fine grains of sand,
Even worse than this problem of supply and demand,
Is the problem of scarcity; I'll help you understand...

OPT OUT!

If Alice has two rocks and Billy Bob has three,
That's five rocks in total, pretty easy to see!
Now imagine that one rock is used to buy fruit,
So one rock times a thousand,
That's some pretty good loot!

And if all through the land, a million rocks had been found,
This Stone Age economy would be prosperous and sound,
But wait! What if Roger dug more rocks from the ground?

Roger went digging, and digging he dug,
   He dug till he found more rocks than he could lug,
   To the market he went, to buy all the fruit,
   And with many rocks to spare, he bought a new suit!

The thing about markets, they're smarter than us,
Big deal! You might say, why all the fuss?
Well the markets know something that you might not see,
That rocks, for example, make bad currency!

For if Roger can cheaply inflate the supply,
Alice's rocks lose their power to buy!
The more rocks there are, the less fruit they're worth,
And there are so very many, rocks here on earth...

Now what do these rocks, have to do with the Dollar?
Well this here is Murray, ask him, he's a scholar!
"Hey Murray! What's wrong with the dollar we use?
It's backed by the government, what can we lose?"
"Hi Alice! Hi Bob! I'll try to explain,
How government money is a runaway train...

So dollars, like rocks, don't mean much, you see,
For the Silly State can print them, and they do so, carefree!
The Silly State prints dollars, all day and all night,
They keep printing dollars, and prices take flight!
The more dollars there are, the less fruit they're worth,
And there are so very many, dollars here on earth...

The State makes you think too, that hoarding is bad,
And if you're not spending, you'll be so very sad!
But hoarding's not bad, in fact, that's just a name,
Hoarding is just saving, it's exactly the same!

Saving is good! We save so we can grow,
Our wealth, our families ˏ you reap what you sow!
If a farmer did sell, all the fruits of her labor,
Without seeds for next year, no one could save her!

And a saver is precisely, what our farmer should be!
To grow more fruit next year, for you and for me!
This all relates to scarcity, which the dollar has not,
Without scarcity, like fruit, your dollars will rot!

The Silly State prints money, more dollars each year,
More money, more dollars, what's there to fear?
Just like Roger's rocks, more money's a bad deal,
When the State prints more money, it's your value they steal!

BRRR...

ONE DOLLAR

E

ven if you save dollars, inside a bank's vault,
They'll lose value each year, and it won't be your fault!
Banks all loan out dollars, more than they take in,
For this reason, I'll take out, my sad violin...

And I'll play you a song, of money gone wrong,
Of fractional lending, and the weak vs. the strong!"
"Murray! We don't want to hear, your violin!
Just tell us, please tell us, how can we win?"
"Fine then! I'll stop!" Murray said with chagrin,
"This, Bob and Alice, is where Bitcoin comes in...

Bitcoin is scarce, and you can't just make more,
For this reason, we often see Bitcoin's price soar,
But as more people use it, the price finds a floor,
No matter how loud, the politicians roar...

They tell us that Bitcoin's for bad guys and thugs!
They tell us that Bitcoin is used to buy drugs!
But criminals prefer dollars, paper money you can't track,
So why then is Bitcoin, under constant attack?

$\mathcal{B}$itcoin, you see, threatens government control,
Bitcoin, in fact, is a power black hole,
It sucks in the power that politicians crave,
And it gives us the power, the power to save!"

"But wait Murray, Bitcoin's too expensive to buy,
I can't afford a whole one, so why should I try?"
"A whole coin sounds nice, but sats are what you need,"
"Sats are Satoshis, right?"
"Yes, Bob, indeed!

Sats are Satoshis, a hundred million to the coin,
Guard your sats fiercely, else a thief will purloin,
But the point here is this, that fractions are okay,
Start stacking sats now, and you'll thank me one day."

"So we keep stacking sats, then what do we do?
Where do we keep them, can we give them to you?"
"The choice here is yours, but here's what I say,
'Not your keys, not your coins,' don't give them away.

If you'd like to use Bitcoin, you need no permission,
And if you'd like to stop Bitcoin, there's no one to petition."
"Murray, wait a sec, what if something goes wrong?
If I mess up a transaction, is that bitcoin just gone?"

"That bitcoin's not gone, it's where you sent it to be,
If you're going to use Bitcoin, responsibility is key,
To be your own bank, there's much you should learn,
But once you learn Bitcoin, you'll keep what you earn."

"But what about in places, where money is tight?
Where speech is restricted all day and all night?
Can Bitcoin help people under violent regimes?
Can Bitcoin help realize their hopes and their dreams?"

"There are so many people with lives that are rough,
But Bitcoin was made for when times there are tough,
I want you to meet my dear friend, Manuela,
She hails from a land that they call Venezuela."

"Hola amigos, les tengo algo que decir,
Que Bitcoin es el futuro, y a la luna se va ir!
Bitcoin me ayuda ahorrar mi dinero,
En mi mente no hay duda, mi porvenir es certero!"

"Bitcoin safeguards her money, Manuela just said,
Because Venezuela's currency is pretty much dead,
The bolivar, like the dollar, has no cap on its supply,
Now add in a tyrant, and the bolivar will die..."

OM...
DO YOUR OWN RESEARCH...
OM...

"Gracias Manuela, thanks Murray!
Now what else should we know?
Where can we buy bitcoin?
Tell us where to go!"
"I can't do it for you, gotta learn on your own!
Do your own research, as the mantra is known.

The great promise of Bitcoin is money that's sound,
Permissionless value, a true common ground,
A world in which people, no matter how small,
Can interact as sovereigns... Once and for all."

~~The End~~

The ₿eginning

Brekkie - The Writer

Jason Don (aka Brekkie von Bitcoin) is Bitcoin artist and advocate based in Los Angeles, California. He believes that sound money is the key to a more prosperous future for all, and that Bitcoin represents the best chance we have at making that future a reality. He currently serves as Creative Director for Swan Bitcoin, but in his off hours, you can usually find him in his studio with a hammer and chisel in his hands and covered head to toe in marble dust.

Flo - The Illustrator

Flo Montoya is a Chilean artist. After going down the rabbit hole in 2017, Flo found creative ways to comunicate the wonders of Bitcoin through different materials and techniques. "Bitcoin values motivate me and strengthen my conviction to be a part of the peaceful revolution of separating money from state".

Simon - Design / Layout Wizard

A man of few words, Simon discovered a love for design. This very same passion has been ignited for him in the Bitcoin world. He now combines both passions and is grateful to be spreading awareness and education around Bitcoin. Simon balances his time working for Swan Bitcoin and Other Alias, his freelance design studio.

Thank You

This book would not have been possible without help. First and foremost, thank you to Satoshi Nakamoto, whoever and wherever you are, for creating Bitcoin and forever changing our lives. To our family and friends who have supported us, even when you did not quite understand Bitcoin yourselves, thank you. We may have been right about Bitcoin, but you were right that we are a little bit crazy. However to quote from Alice in Wonderland, we will tell you a secret: "All the best people are." You may not understand Bitcoin yet, but we still love you and thank you for having an open mind to this crazy, amazing thing that drives us inexorably forward- Bitcoin.

This book would also not have been possible without the help of the Bitcoin community. Thank you for your support and your friendship.

For reading early drafts and sharing your wisdom and feedback and for supporting us at all stages of the book's development, we would like to thank the following individuals:

Michael Caras aka The Bitcoin Rabbi

Yan Pritzker

Brady Swenson

Cory Klippsten

Marc Weinstein

Christian Keroles

Michael Oshins

Nik Bhatia

Matthew Kaye

Nathaniel Whittemore

Stephan Livera

Gigi

Phil Geiger

Pierre Rochard

Michael Goldstein

Saifedean Ammous

Stephanie & Irving Don

Alex Don

Nicole Don

Domingo Donoso

Gonzalo Montoya

Gabriela Salvadores

Francisca Montoya

Ioram Jacubovsky

Javier Montoya

Javier Bastardo

Debbie, Oli & Jack